Fangs

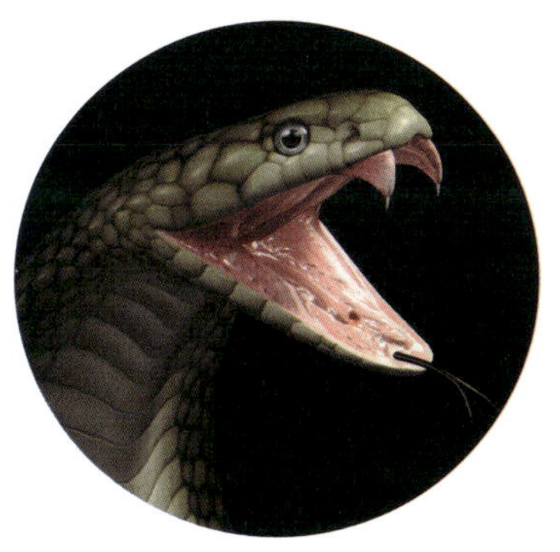

Written by
Stephen Rickard

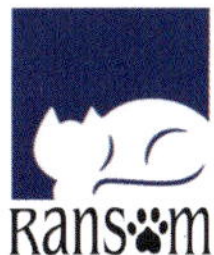

Ransom

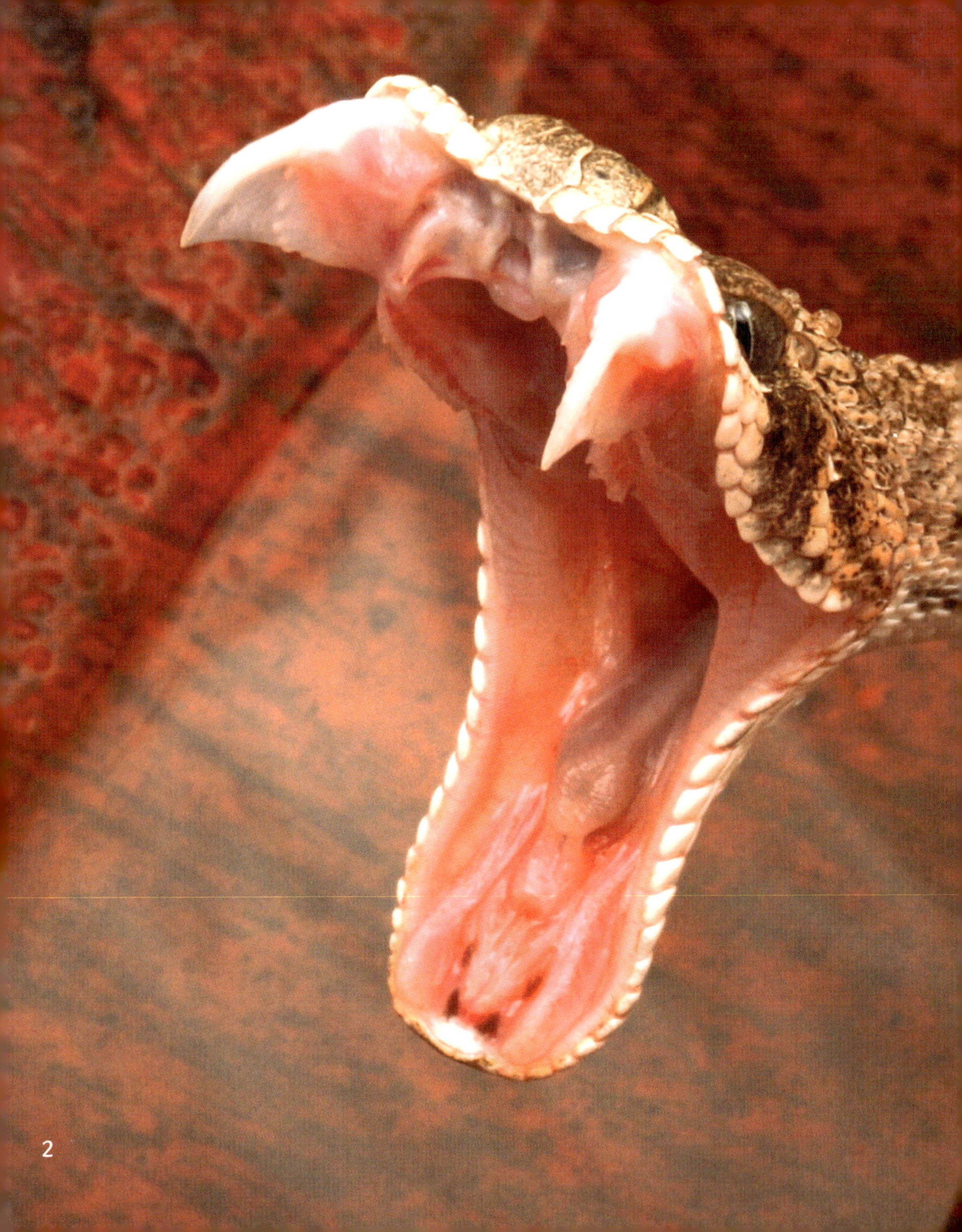

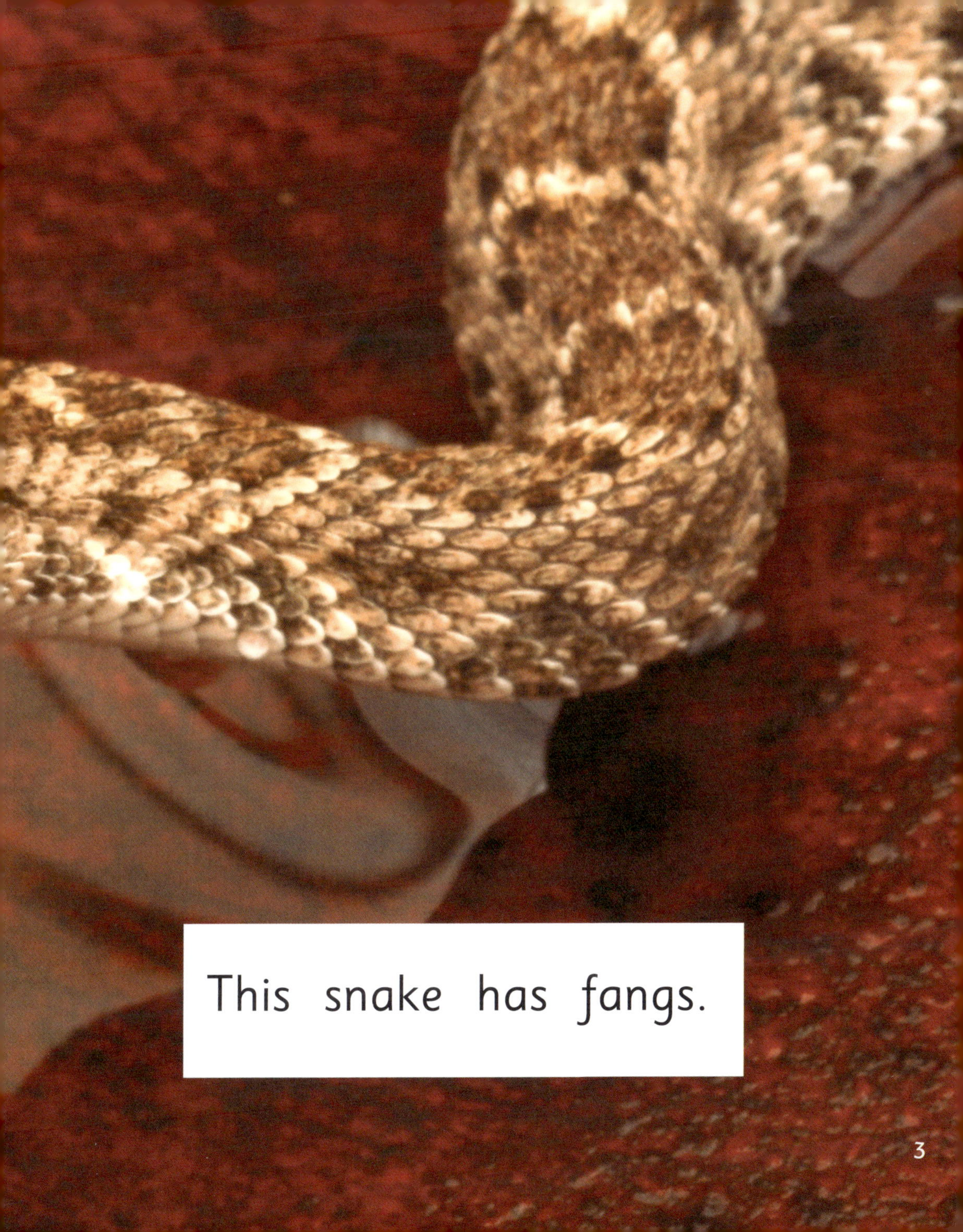

This snake has fangs.

This cat has fangs.

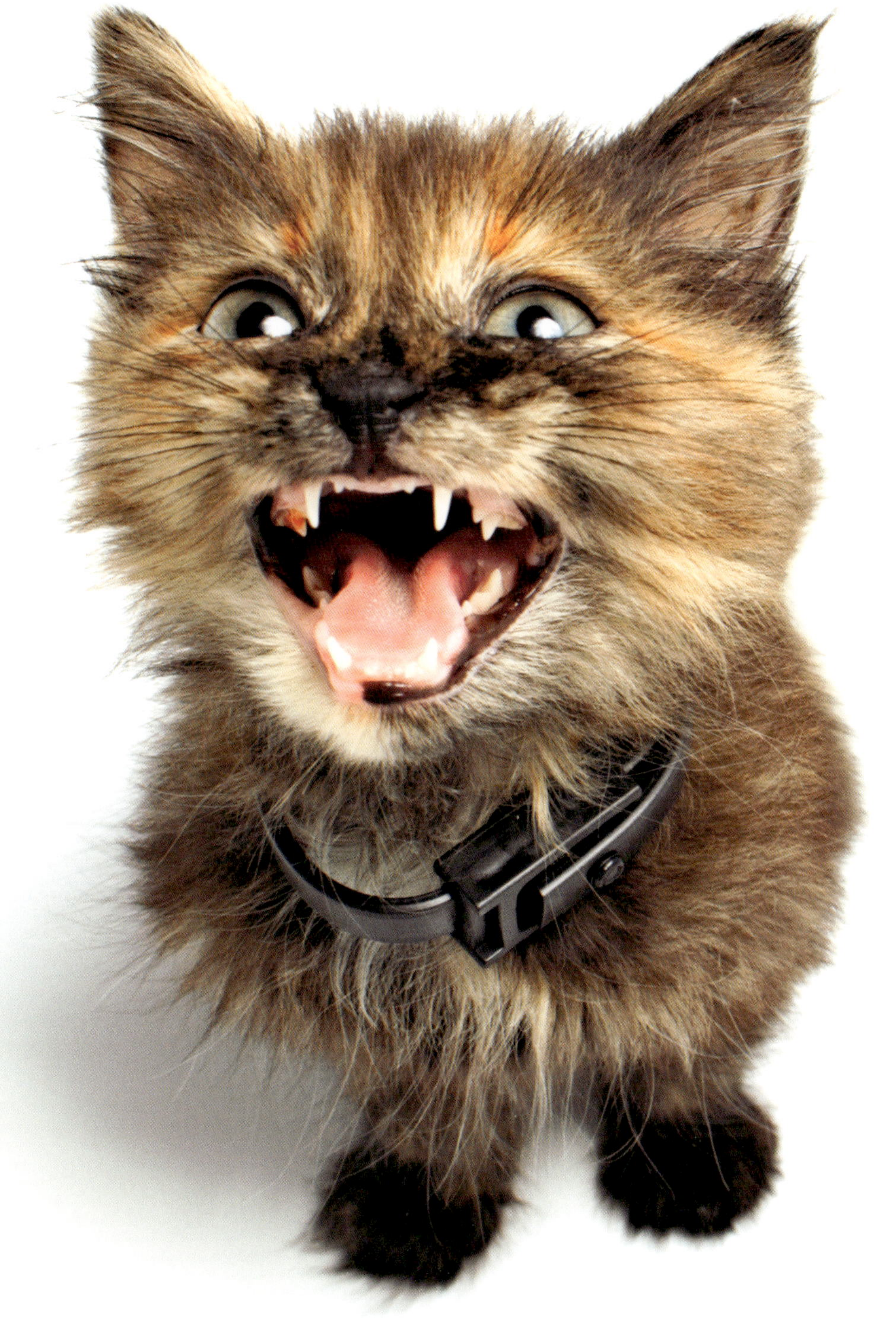

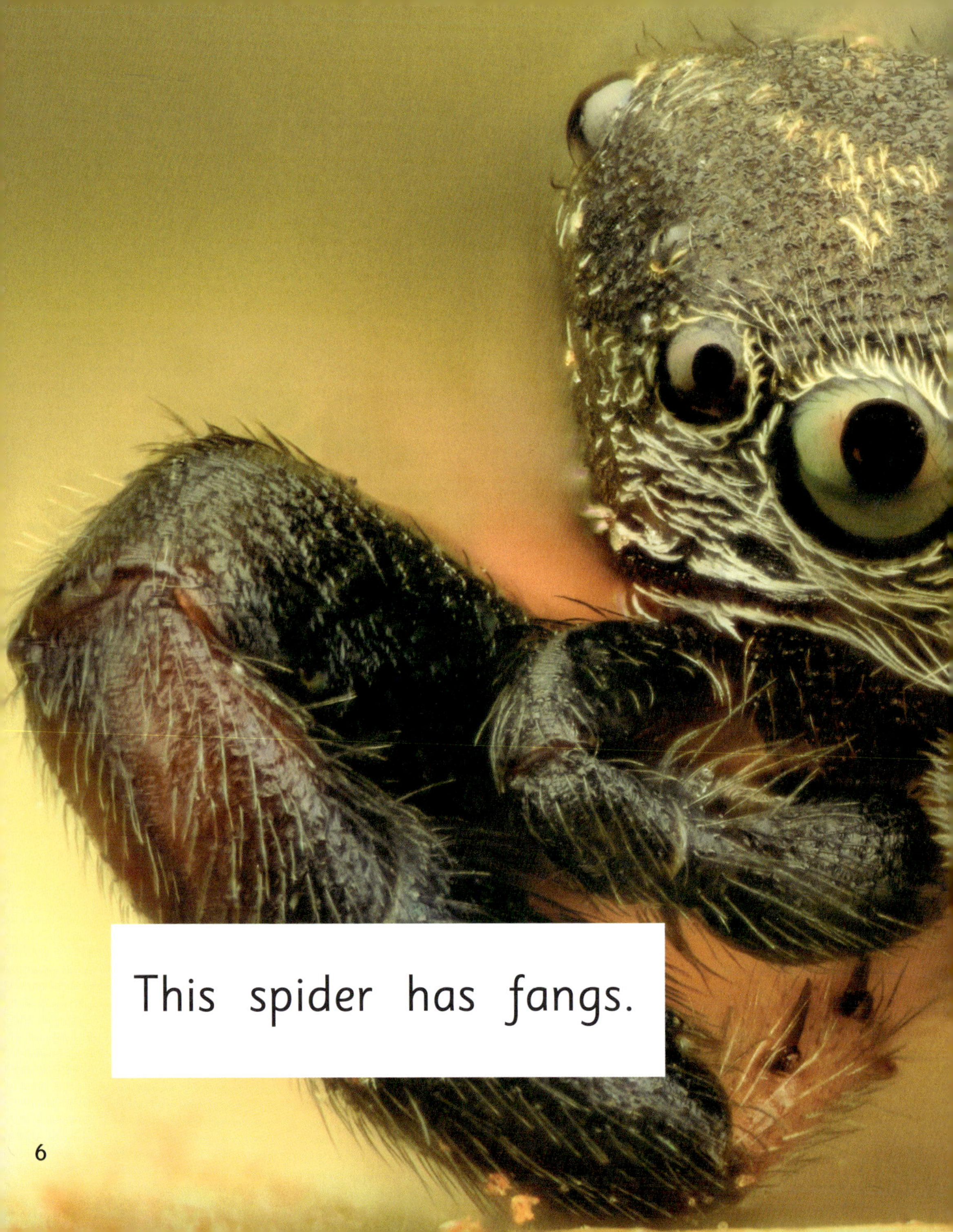

This spider has fangs.

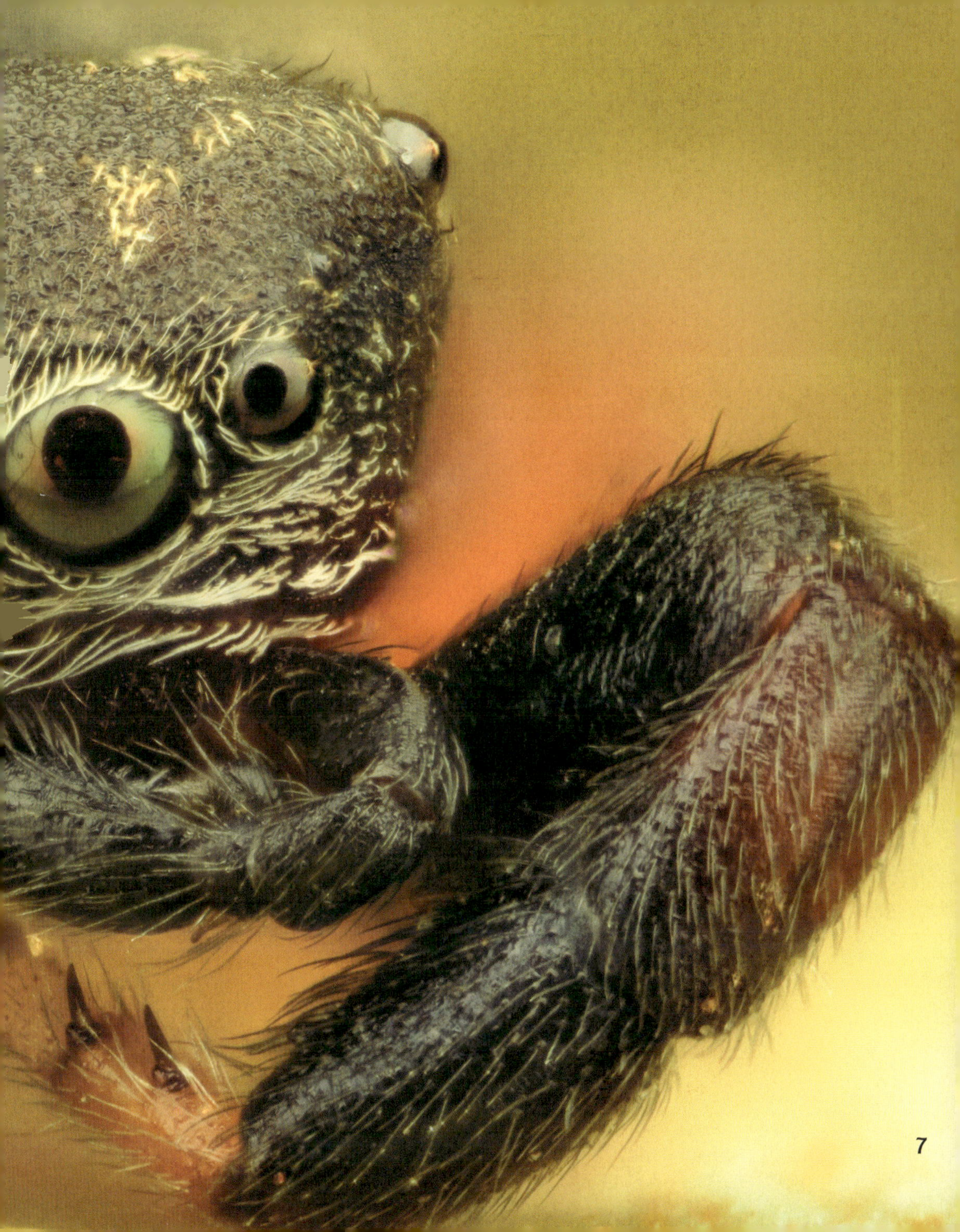

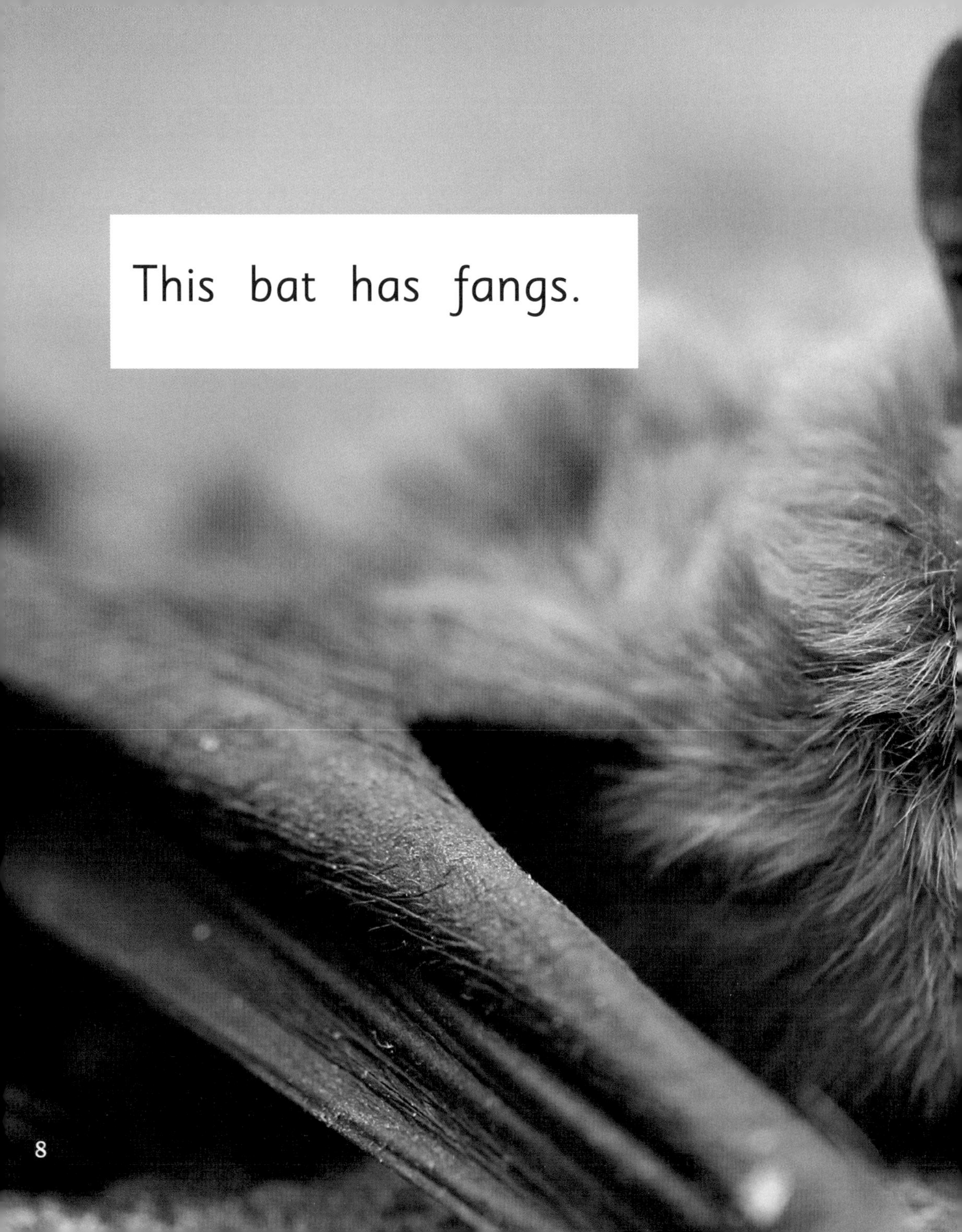

This bat has fangs.

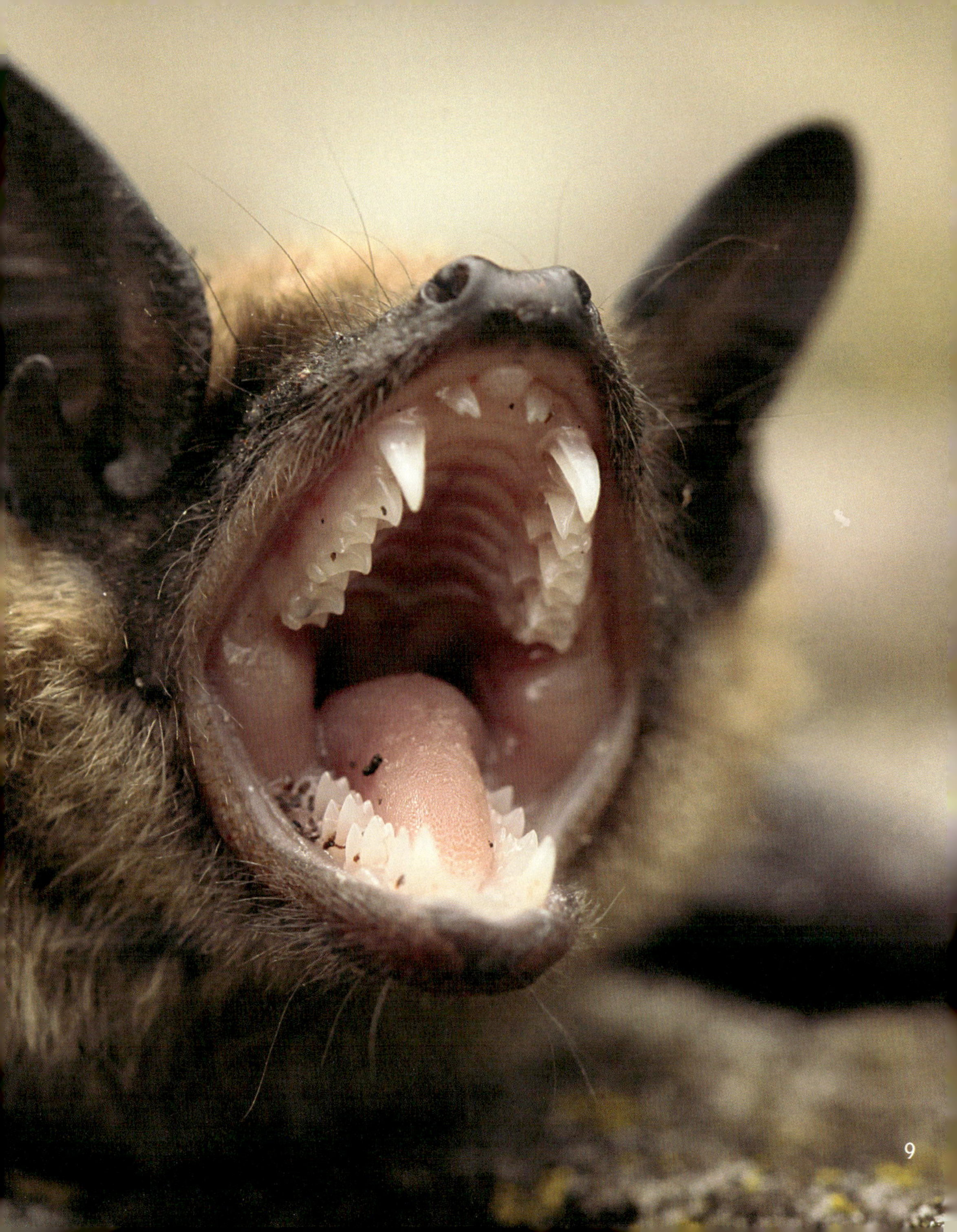

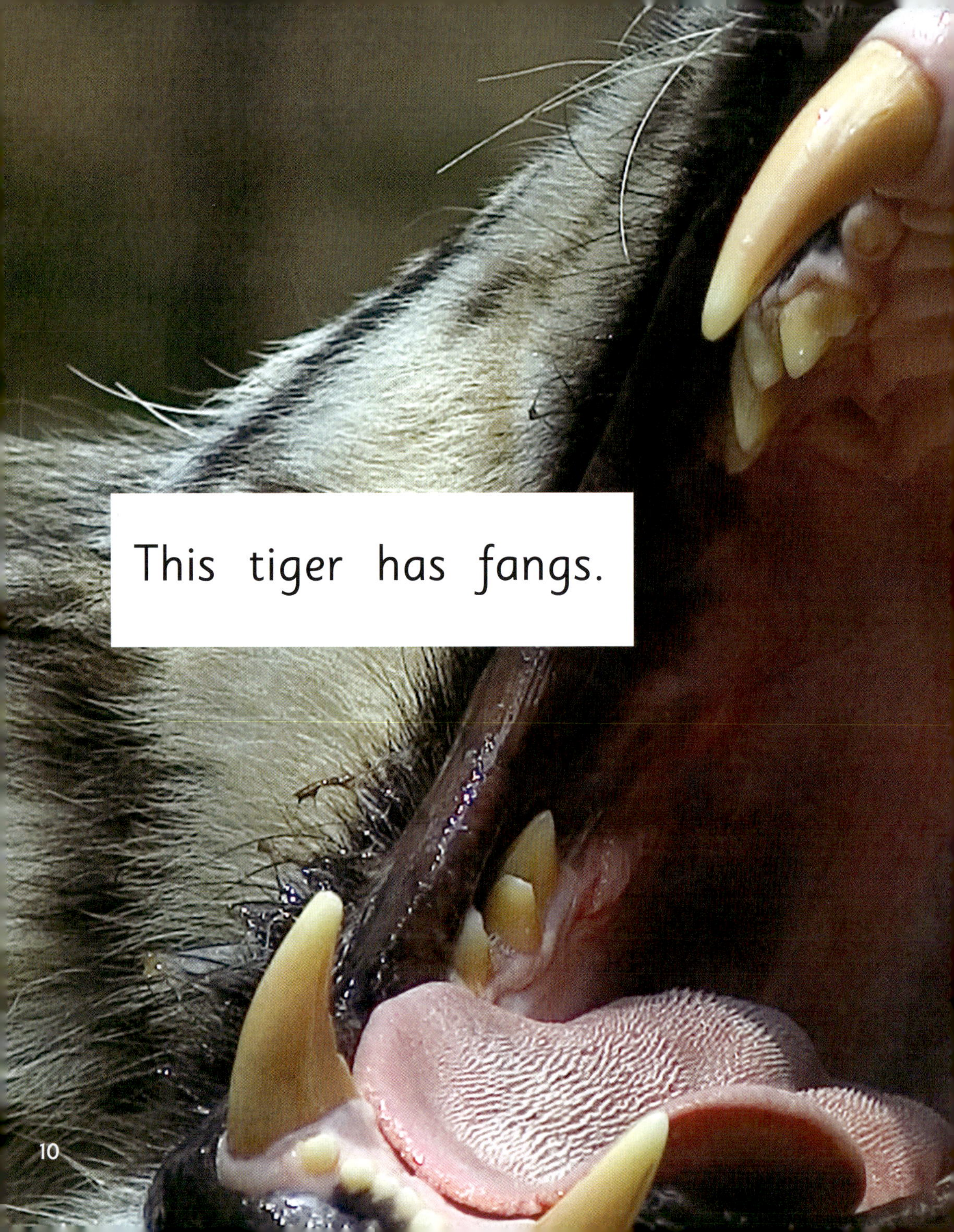
This tiger has fangs.